CW00503253

CUCKOLD CONVERSION KIT - FOR WIVES

Ethically Getting Him To Want And Need A Tiny Cuck Status

ALLORA SINCLAIR

Cuckoo
Publishing

CUCKOLD CONVERSION KIT - For Wives

©2021 by Allora Sinclair

Front Cover Illustration by: pressmaster

WHAT'S IN IT FOR ME?

I suspect this book is in your hands by one of two means. A - You are proactively seeking a way to help move your hubby along the cuckold scale so you can achieve greater control and freedom in your own life, or B - Your hubby has suggested you read this to help you accentuate his experience as your little cucky boy. Either way, you're here to enhance Bob, Bill, Tom, Dick, or Harry's experience and journey into being cuckolded. IF hubby is still in the dark (which statistically is very unlikely) and you want to become a cuckoldress, you need to first establish if going down this path is even a viable option.

Does your husband have the DNA of a cuckold? If this book was given to you, the answer is already a resounding "YES!". If you picked up this book on your own, looking for suggestions in an already established cuck relationship, again, the answer is likely a "HELL YA!". If hubby does not know what the hell cuckolding is but you do, you need to tread lightly. Being a "man" is deeply ingrained in the male psyche. If your husband has no cuckold tendencies, YOU CAN NOT CONVERT HIM, period, full stop.

I intended this book for those that have already established that your male partner is indeed a cuckold. Perhaps he is struggling with the transition or you are struggling with how far you can take things and are looking for some practical advice. If so, this book is perfect for you. If you have run out of ideas but sense your little cucky boy is enjoying your life as a cuckold couple, again, this book will do you well.

I do not intend it as a manual to help wives flip their men into becoming a compliant little sissy. If the thought of cuckolding at any level makes your husband sick to his stomach, raging mad, or feeling unwelcomed angst, I cannot help you. You are doomed to a life of vanilla or perhaps swinging in a best case. If you're looking to play with other men and you see cuckolding as the perfect vehicle to do so BUT your husband is not on board - be very careful. You are heading towards cheating on your husband. Seek a counselor. Your marriage/relationship is on the rocks and failure to get outside help will almost guarantee a dissolved marriage.

With that all out of the way, I want to welcome you into the sisterhood. Being a Cuckoldress is both empowering and filled with pleasure. It is also a lot of work. You have a cuckold husband and they are a righteous, demanding little group of boys. They want what they can not have. Their minds are on turbo charge 24/7. I would argue they are blessed with the biggest sex organ of anyone - their weak/sick little minds.

They can't just have sex for the fun of sex. They need more. A LOT MORE. Just as you have a libido that craves proper service, they have the same insatiable libido. The problem is their libido is not between their legs. It sits on their shoulders. Therein lies the problem and the function this book aims to serve.

Consider this book to be a top tips and tricks to make your cucky a happy little girl, while ensuring your needs in every aspect are taken care of. Simply having sex with other men is great, but for a cuckold, they want you to take things further. They want you to humiliate them, manipulate them, and control them (in a discrete but consensual way). Having other sex partners helps, but it is just the icing on the cake. The truly successful cuckold couple excels in this mutual understanding that sex is just the payoff. The genuine joy and love you feel together as a couple starts well before. With the assumption that you already understood cuckold dynamics, let's dive into some specific actionable steps you can take to help stress and improve the quality of your relationship with your cuckold.

STEP 1 - NO PAIN, NO GAIN

W ith a few exceptions, cuckolds love
emotional pain. The more emotional pain
that is bestowed upon them, the more they
worship you. You must understand this is EMOTIONAL
PAIN only. Moreover, this is emotional pain that is laser-
focused on anything to do with sexuality and their
manhood.

Telling your cuckold that he is useless at his full-time
job at work is likely not going to accomplish much, other
than be hurtful and mean-spirited. Telling him he is utterly
useless in satisfying you in bed is the complete opposite;
it's one of the most loving, kind things you could say
to him.

This can be a lot for a new cuckoldress to get her head
around: Do this under this circumstance, but under that
circumstance, don't? Yip. These men we have fallen in love
with are one very complicated group. Speaking from my

experience, davie has been the most amazing man I've ever known. I feel like a goddess all day, every day. But I've also felt stretched to my limits, trying to understand his mind. Frustrated, fed-up, and, at times, annoyed.

Cuckolds are like a bunch of teenage girls in the middle of their monthly hormone cycle. One minute they're up, then they're down. They need, need, need. Then they give everything they have to make you happy, even if it's at their own expense.

Learning to manage their mood swings is the first and most important tool you'll need. Once you learn to tap into the cuckold mind, both your worlds stabilize, providing for fun, love, and excitement beyond each of your wildest dreams.

It all starts with a deep understanding that you can do no wrong. With that, you can not provide too much pain if it surrounds your sexuality or his manhood. We'll keep this as our little secret, but cuckolds love being pushed - even when they say they don't. The caveat to this is the hard lines established. If they have expressed a hard limit, never cross that limit. Never. However, I encourage you to push to the very max of their limits, leaving nothing but air between your words/actions and their limit being crossed.

Examples of what I'm saying, you ask?

Your cuck says he wants no kissing between you and your bull. Okay, don't kiss... on the lips. BUT, make sure to kiss EVERY OTHER PART of the magnificent bull's body - especially around his neck, ears, and chest.

Your cuck says he does not want you to have sex with your bull bareback. Okay. But nothing says you can't swallow every ounce. Maybe telling him how much you would love to do it, but only in discussion. You're not crossing the line, but you're as close as one can get.

The point is to always push the envelope. The deeper and more frequently you push, the more your cuckold will reward you.

In the early stages of cuckolding, it's very common for both the cuck and the cuckoldress to be shy in expressing what they like. I'm here to tell you cuck's love the emotional pain. The more pain you give them, the more gain they make in moving forward in feeling happy and fulfilled. Hearing this, I suspect should offer some excitement for you as well.

A true cuckoldress likes to inflict pain. This is your chance. I know, feels too good to be true, right? This is exactly why most cuckold couples have deeper, more loving, and lasting relationships than the average vanilla couple. They drop the gloves and embrace it.

Circling back in the dialogue, the most straightforward concept that will run the balance of this book - no pain, no gain. If you want to learn to help your little cucky grow into a kind, gentle, loving, and loyal princess, push. Don't doubt yourself. Don't hold back. As you continue down the path, this concept becomes natural, but at first, it is a bit of a mind-bender.

"I want my cuckold to know I love him and I want him to stop getting all emotional" The answer: If you want to gain in your cuckold dynamic relationship, you need to inflict emotional pain.

STEP 2 - STICKS AND STONES

⚬ℛℚ

But names will never hurt me? Um, NO! Your words carry more power with a cuckold than any actions. It is the biggest oversight that any cuckold material I've looked at has missed. The power of your words 10X any bull you could have in any setting under any circumstances.

Cuckolds are all about the mind fuck. Yes, this is somewhat of an oversimplification but the reality is they love to be fucked in the mind NOT the bed. What exactly does this mean? It means your little cucky is constantly just one level below horny at all times. Everything you say has the potential to turn them on. In the bedroom, over the phone at work, in the grocery store, while you are clipping your toenails. If you say the right things, you flip their switch.

I know it's one of those "aha" moments, right? Your cuckold partner, who is the same guy that shows no outward sexual aggression, has a higher internal sex drive than the most animalistic bull you have ever been with. It's true. The problem is, a cuckold's sex drive is focused on their thoughts, not their genitals.

What you say or don't say has incredible power. The question you must ask is "what do I say?".

As much as humanly possible, you want to criticize, condemn, humiliate and belittle him... IN ANY WAY THAT PERTAINS TO HIS MANHOOD, MASCULINITY, OR SEXUAL PROWESS. NEVER, take this into who he is as a person. They are very distinct and different parts of who he is and one should not cross into the other.

If Billy/Bobby/Joe or whoever has upset you, be careful how you respond. Telling him he's a terrible person or stupid or a loser (contrary to popular belief in this lifestyle) it is not the way to go. You need to respond in ways that attack his manhood, not his personhood.

Examples?

Instead of saying he's a jerk or an asshole, telling him, he's a wimp, a sissy, or a useless princess – this kind of response not only will get an almost immediate apology. It will also get full compliance from him and you have also just played with his little pee-pee.

Try to imagine the power this kind of shift can have on your relationship. Just shifting your words towards his lack of masculinity or sexuality is a game-changer. AND THIS IS APPLICABLE EVEN WHEN YOU'RE NOT UPSET WITH HIM.

The point of this book is to help you guide and manage your cuckold, so you both enjoy the dynamic. This little shift is likely the biggest and most effective long-term action you can take that will edge you both straight into a vibrant and satisfying relationship.

The more you can cut him down, humiliate him, embarrass him about not being a real man, the more and the deeper his love and worship of you will blossom. Just be careful to not cross the line and start degrading him as a person. Always keep your words focused on his manhood.

Davie has had many cranky moments where I've lost my patience. From time to time, I've made my scorn about him and his actions... WRONG! As soon as I flip to making it about him being a useless little girl or told him he needs to stop trying to be all macho and accept his lack of a working pee-pee, he instantly smiles, gets all soft, and begs for forgiveness. It's hilarious once you see how easy it is to get your way.

Just remember, he craves this way of being treated. The more you do this, the deeper and stronger his attraction to following the cuckolding path becomes. The more you do this, the more you get your way, the more you are treated the way you deserve to be treated (like a Goddess) and frankly, it's actually a lot of fun once you get used to it and get past the random guilty feelings.

Sticks and stones are overrated. Your words don't hurt. They help. Keep consistent and don't be afraid to deliver nasty condemnation often. Just make sure it's never about him as a person. It's always about him as a man (or lack thereof). You can thank me by having your husband read the companion book to this.

STEP 3 - MATERIAL GIRL

A cuckold loves everything girly. They relate to the girly girl and all her sweet and lovely high-maintenance ways. As a cuckoldress, being "one of the boys" is not your jam. A cuck loves the feminine. If your relationship has you both doing "guy things" like going to the football game or sharing a beer while you're fishing... it has to stop.

Not for you, silly. For him. You want to close down any outlets he has that develop his manliness. Often, this may mean you too need to shut down some activities that are on the masculine side but hear me out.

Billy/Bobby/Stevie has two potential scenarios. He and you can go to a baseball game together OR, you can tell him you want to use that money to buy a new sexy outfit and you need that time to go to the hair salon to get your hair and nails done... BECAUSE you want to look sexy for your bull.

Number one, you've just denied him of a guy thing (the more you do that, the quicker he will make a full transition to a sweet little cucky) AND you have pampered yourself to have fun and turn heads.

Number two, this is a selfish act on your behalf. All in the name of making yourself look and feel sexier for others. That is a whole separate topic, but suffice to say you end up with a win-win-win situation.

It seems counter-intuitive, but it is far from it. The whole cuckold dynamic is counter-intuitive/up-side-down and backward from how we all used to think. Trying to understand it would be nice but the reality is it just works that way. Accept it and embrace it.

Cuckolds are drawn to women that exude high sexual energy. It's not thought out like that, it just happens that way. Just like cuckoldresses tend to seek men that are perhaps power players in the "real world" but they have a soft, feminine side that can be easily manipulated with little effort. Did you think of your partner this way before you got together? Likely not. BUT, in retrospect, I'm sure you can agree you kind of knew you had a man that you could mold into whatever you wanted... You just never thought that you would.

Don't for one second think your cuck appreciates you fitting in with his guy ways. He sees a Goddess. He wants to treat you like a goddess and he wants you to expect such treatment. If you aren't materialistic, I strongly encourage you to think again.

The more you demand to have every aspect of your life pampered, the more it will drive him crazy with love, adoration, and believe it or not, lust. Just the simple act of wanting more. More make-up, more visits to the hair salon, more massages, more trips to exotic destinations, more anything that puts you up on a pedestal.

Push this as far as your budget can afford (without being irresponsible). Being economical and getting the no-name brand pair of high-heeled shoes is great if that's all you can afford. However, if your family budget allows for the Louboutin's, get them - even if they are not worth it. Why? Because you are a Goddess. Make him feel it in the pocketbook and the head.

I always get concerned readers may think I'm suggesting I support Findom. I do not. But cuckolding is largely a mind game that thrives in disparity. Being dominant and insisting you deserve the best, most up-to-date is the very least he can do to ensure your elevated status as a Goddess. It makes the imbalance that much more real. In turn, it enhances the feelings you both love - being spoiled and sexy while he feels deprived but grateful to be in your presence. Everyone wins in a cuckold relationship when you stop feeling guilty and embrace the material girl.

STEP 4 - WHEN OPPORTUNITY KNOCKS

♂♀

A s a cuckold couple, your lives will be somewhat "off the grid" to the normal vanilla population. I remember feeling like davie and I were part of some kind of secret society. In a way, you are. But that does not mean you can't have lots of fun in the vanilla world without compromising your privacy to judgy eyes.

Whenever the urge hits, don't be afraid to use your sexual energy to boost your ego and make cucky a thrilled man. This does not have to be an all the time, every second of the day kind of thing, but the more you do it, the more you both have fun. Lots of fun.

What the hell am I talking about? Flirting. Both by how you dress and/or by what you say and do.

This is a "works every time" situation. Whether you're by yourself or together as a couple. If you're going to work (so you are not with each other) don't be afraid to flirt. If you can, dress as provocatively as the setting will permit.

I'm not suggesting you wear clubwear at the office, but you can certainly wear that tight pantsuit or the jeans that make your backside look just that little more... appealing. Maybe your top fits tastefully but shows your curves just that bit more than a run-of-the-mill blouse.

Remember ladies, flirting is NOT cheating. Even more so, it's welcomed as a special treat if you embellish the experience with your little cucky when you get home. Don't be afraid to be "friendly". Ya never know if that young trainee may come in handy one day down the road.

The real pay-off is when your little cucky is with you. I love this, especially when davie and I have to go to the hardware store or someplace dominated by the male specimen. I always make a point of losing the track pants and sweatshirt and jump into my short shorts or T-shirt that I have oh-so innocently forgot to put a bra on underneath.

I make sure davie understands he is to remain silent unless spoken to. When I'm speaking to "Ken" or "Adam" or whatever his name tag says, I always make sure to be overly thankful. Perhaps a gentle touch on his arm. Maybe a wink. My tone is soft and gentle, always making sure he knows I respect him as a man, all the while referring to davie as useless with the man jobs.

I swear I see a bulge in davie's pants as we stand at the check-out. And, here's the real pay-off. Davie loves when I do this. I'm fairly sure the sales associate doesn't mind the subtle ego-stroking and almost seductive tone in my body language and tone of voice. And I come away feeling like I own both men. Talk about power.

The point is, you want to play this kind of thing out as much as possible. Yes, there will be times where you just want to get that loaf of bread and go home. You're in your scrubby clothes and you don't care. That's okay. But whenever you have the opportunity, use it. Flirt till it hurts. To quote a John Cougar Song "It Hurts So Good".

Be mindful of the opportunities that lie outside the hotel or the sex club. You can play without playing, at least with your little cuck's mind. It has so much power that goes under the radar of many cuckold couples. I would not suggest that you go over the top and start getting phone numbers. Just the innocent flirt that has everyone scratching their head wondering if it was their imagination or were you indeed flirting.

I should also add that not only can this be fun for both you and your cuck, it also speeds up your little cuckolds' desire to be more attentive to your every need, compliant to your every request, and be deeply grateful that you are even with him. Try it. I think it will pleasantly surprise you at its power.

STEP 5 - ALWAYS !

This is a big one that is more of a long-term point of view. Consider it a bit of a game but in reality, it serves more as a training guideline for your relationship health down the road. Always... try to get your way. Always!

But. But. But, what if he wants to watch golf and you want to watch a TV version of Phantom of the Opera? Say bye-bye to the golf. You want the Cherry Chunk ice cream and he wants the Rocky Road? I guess Cherry Chunk it is. Always assume you are to get your way.

If that means your wants are the same as his wants, then let him have it. But only because you wanted that outcome. Otherwise... did I mention, Always get your way?

I appreciate I'm being a little off the cuff in the above but for a reason. A cuckoldress has a lot of responsibility.

As much as it is rewarding and I believe the most satisfying way any woman could choose to live, it still is demanding. You may love the lifestyle but you still had to make a significant amount of changes in your life and your values to make things make sense.

The payoff is your cuckold has elevated you to a God-like status. You deserve this. I genuinely believe it is not a privilege, it's your right. Do you think you should compromise? Never ever ever. You are a Goddess. Your cuckold wants to feel that you own that status. He longs to feel you own him. Not just his little pee-pee. Not just his wallet. He wants you to own his soul. Seriously. The closer you both get to you mutually understanding you own his soul, the deeper your love for each other will be.

Always getting your way is a gentle reminder of that fact. You own him. You own his wants and needs. I know this seems extreme but I assure you, as you evolve, you will both ultimately end with this conclusion. It is quite empowering for both of you. But it is a tremendous responsibility. You hold his life in your hands. You deserve some perks for that, no?

With all that said, for obvious reasons, if you have a life-changing decision then his input should hold equal weight to your own; Raising children and all the fun parenting that comes with it - this is a team effort. You both should share in who gets what in the decisions that are made.

When it's your everyday mundane life choices, always get your way.

But what if cucky doesn't want to bend and comply with your request? First off, learn that nothing is a request if it comes from you. It's not a suggestion. It's not open for a debate. It is your expectations. It's happening, end of discussion - no matter what it is.

If it is still met with resistance, punishment is necessary. "But isn't that just mean and cruel?" You ask?

STEP 6 - PUNISHMENT

∞

Oh, the pain! Wait, what? Not physical pain before you get ahead of yourself.

Let me remind you ladies that cuckolds are all about being emotionally tortured. They crave to feel sorrow, angst, and shame. They are masochistic in the highest and most eloquent way. Likewise, this section should excite you as well. A true cuckoldresss has a sadistic side that rarely gets acknowledged or expressed so overtly as in the world of cuckold punishment.

To remove a little negative stigma to the name, let's call punishment more like a type of cuckold training. If cucky does not comply with a request, he needs to learn. He needs to have ingrained in him you are a Goddess and compromise is not on the table. Not today. Not tomorrow. Not any day. Your wish needs to become his command.

Again, to be taken with a grain of salt here. If it's a life-altering event, obviously, you both need to pause the cuckold lifestyle to deal with the crises or whatever. But if things are status quo, there is no negotiation. You get your way ALWAYs.

Failure to understand or act accordingly needs to result in some form of repercussions. This is where the fun gets real. Particularly knowing that he longs for such training but was afraid to ask.

This is where your words and your actions should cross. Nothing hurts a cuck more than being told you want to stop cuckolding him. He wants to be cuck'd. It runs deep into his veins. I would leave this as a last resort but that's your go-to if everything else seems unsuccessful.

I found the most effective way to train davie requires some advanced thought. I know what outfits turn his crank the most. I also know the look he loves to see me having, just as I'm going to see a bull. That "oh my God, I want to fuck your brains out, but I respect I'm not good enough" look comes over his face. He struggles to keep his hands off of me. The outfits that solicit the look, that hunger he has... I make sure I'm dressed for it.

Then I tease him. Tease him till he is begging. Often suggesting tonight I might let him have some special "treat". Just when he thinks he's gonna be a lucky little girl, I shut him down and change into the old ratty clothes, remove my makeup and sit on the couch watching Netflix ignoring him. When he asks "wtf?", I then tell him he is being punished. If he ever wants a piece of me ever again, he needs an attitude adjustment.

To be clear, from that point, I never change my mind. No matter what he says or does, I stand my ground for the balance of the day. The next time he tries to disobey, the memories of this kind of event come flooding back quicker than you would think.

Another workaround that serves a similar function is the cock cage. Leaving it on longer than originally agreed or discussed. What a wonderful idea. Just be careful. It can be problematic if all he knows is a locked life. It is also problematic as it is very effective but can lead to removal being postponed time and time again. Too much of that can break any cuckold - and not in a good way.

You want the whole thing to be an exciting and fun learning experience. Don't forget, however, it is a balancing act. You want to give your cucky emotional pain. Using sexuality or lack of it is wonderful. But too much of this method is destructive and quickly breaks any loving bonds you have.

I want to remind you, the point of punishment is primarily to help grow a deeper cuckold dynamic with your princess. Punishment meets that goal but it is not the end goal. It is a means to an end.

If done right, your cuckold will flower as your little cuck, making your life wonderfully magical. It also helps satisfy his needs to feel used and abused. Controlled and manipulated, all in the name of disparity. Just don't overdo whatever needs to be done.

STEP 7 - CROSS THE LINE

No, I'm not talking about crossing the line of whatever you and your partner have established as hard boundaries. I'm referring to lines of the vanilla world. This ties into two other steps mentioned earlier; When opportunity knocks and punishment.

Most of a cuckolding lifestyle is done in the privacy of your own home, sex club, or with a bull. Taking the dynamic out into the vanilla world can be scary and intimidating (for both of you). However, if done right, it carries more weight than in any other venue.

Publicly humiliating your cuck in front of the vanilla world can feel too much. Depending on what it is, it very well may be. HOWEVER, doing things with tact and in subtle ways can be extremely effective. Calling your cucky a princess at the check-out might be over the top. Calling him baby... not so much. It's one of those "is she being cute? Sexy? Insulting?" Ya just don't know. Yet to your cuck, you're removing his manhood. No real man wants to be considered a baby.

This is the kind of thing you want to work at. Admittedly, it's hard to not cross lines but as you'll learn to discover, most folks don't give it too much thought unless it's something extreme.

The one I love is sissy. I know it drives davie nuts when I tell him to stop being such a sissy. I make sure that we are not in too compromised a situation, but sometimes, I'll let it slip. He gets all embarrassed. I get a few looks. But it's not too harsh yet diminishes his manhood completely.

As already mentioned, flirting in the vanilla world is the best. This is something I encourage all you ladies to consider deeply. When it is done openly in the vanilla world (especially after I've just emasculated davie by calling him a sissy or such a wimp) then turning to the real man... yum. I feel so empowered that I have both men's balls in the palm of my hands and both are enjoying it for completely different reasons.

The result is a cucky that can barely control himself as we get to the car.

The crucial point I want to drive home here is the importance of taking some of your cuckolding dynamic out into the streets. Don't keep this relationship all tucked away in the privacy of your secret world. Yes, it can cause some awkward moments between you and other men/women - your cuck will love it, regardless. But it has also created a few surprising moments of bonding with other women.

At least three times I've been approached by other women that have commented how impressed they are that I have trained my hubby so well. The unspoken look in their eyes suggests they, too, have a similar lifestyle dynamic. It's a sort of bonding moment between women that supports each other.

Making your dynamic public needs to be done with caution but please consider how exponentially effective it can be to you, your cuck, and in rare instances, to other women that need a role model.

STEP 8 - I WANT THAT

✦

Never hold back in expressing your needs and desires. The cuckoldress is sadistic. Own it. Love it. Embrace it. With that comes a degree of pleasure you experience when you know you have inflicted a degree of pain on your cuckold. He in turn loves to have that pain.

What better way to accomplish both by not holding back on your needs as selfish and self-centered as they may be. The more selfish they are, the better. ESPECIALLY if it is at your cuck's expense.

This includes what you want materially and sexually.

You want that outfit. You want that trip to Hedonism II. You need your breasts enlarged. You want to fuck that guy over there. You need this guy to pay attention to you.

The more you openly demand to your cuckold, the better. Perhaps being overly dramatic here, but if every sentence you spoke was a need, want or demand - your cuckold would want to be in conversation with you all day long.

If you take only one thing from this entire book. Just one thing. It would be that a cuckold's biggest turn on is your desires. They want you TO WANT TO FUCK OTHER GUYS and they want you TO WANT TO EMOTIONALLY AND SEXUALLY HURT THEM - the more YOU WANT IT, the more they're placed in complete and utter ecstasy.

This is so key and is so so so undervalued in cuckold relationships. You can do do do whatever the hell you want, but if you're doing it to please your cuck, it's not worth very much. If you're doing it BECAUSE IT'S WHAT YOU ACTUALLY WANT/DESIRE/NEED, it is a major power play.

Make sure, at every possible intersection, you vocalize your wants.

If you're new to cuckolding, this is one of the hardest obstacles you will cross. It will be easier to just "do him" than to say YOU **WANT TO** "DO HIM". Trust me, saying it and meaning it is the magic powder to take your little cucky's world into outer space.

Will it hurt him and his ego? Absolutely.

Will he love it and love you even more BECAUSE you had the guts to not just do it but rather say it? 100% guaranteed. Notice I've said nothing with such conviction - to guarantee you something. Here, I'm that confident.

IF YOUR HUSBAND IS A CUCKOLD, this is the number one, most important, and effective thing you can do to crank everything up to 11. No questions asked. No sub notes or "it depends on" footnotes.

Why?

Rewinding to the beginning, cuckolds are all about mind fuck and emotional pain. This is the holy grail of fucking with their minds and inflicting emotional pain. There are many things about becoming a cuckoldress that are a challenge to understand or adapt to, even if it's what you want. I have found the humiliation and intentional enforcement of a disparity for me was the hardest.

But, even harder than that was vocalizing it to davie. I love being selfish, pampered, treated like a goddess. I love having the complete freedom to play with anybody my heart desires and to know it makes davie happy too. And I want all of it.

Letting him know I wanted it took courage. Way more than it did to just play with my stable of bulls.

Why?

Because I feared that letting him know it was no longer a little sex game we played, that I wanted this lifestyle for us... I wanted it. I was terrified that it would make the "game" finally stop being a game. That it could put our marriage in jeopardy.

In retrospect, I can tell you it did stop any feelings of our lifestyle as being a game. It became a reality that it was not something we just did... it became the final step to actualize who we are as a cuckold couple. To that end, it was the best, most positive thing I ever did. It did not threaten our marriage. It strengthened it tenfold.

The take-away is stopping! Stop holding back on what you want and start telling your cucky all your wants. The more a Goddess asks, the more a Goddess gets. It is that simple.

STEP 9 - SCULTPTING CLASSES

A cuckold relationship is a dynamic relationship. It is a relationship that is in constant change. Every encounter. Every point of humiliation. Every demand for a household chore to be done.

As a couple, you go through periods of shifting that change you as individuals and change you as a couple. How you looked going into the lifestyle will look substantially different after ten or fifteen years.

You will morph into a woman that is in control, and having an openly self-confident air about you. You will not settle for "good enough" in most areas of your life. People outside the lifestyle will sit up and take notice. You'll find many compliments come your way.

Statements like "Allora, you've changed. You're just so... I don't know what it is, but I like it. I never noticed you before but now I kinda look up to you." (And yes that's an actual quote from a close friend of mine that was unaware of davie and my cuckold status). But then you'll also get the statements like; "How did you do it? What's your secret for gaining so much... pizazz?" People get nosy. How you handle that is a question of choice.

With your little girl cucky, they become softer, less challenging to you or anyone else. They tend to take a back seat in social settings (in the vanilla world) and most notably they become devout followers and attentive to your every need. They truly worship you. To them, you become their god. Yes, this is a wee bit intimidating, especially knowing the complete power and control you have over their every step.

HOWEVER, this is a long-range view of where you both are going. In the meantime, you are not there. As a cuckoldress, you are the driver. You already know how it's going to turn out. Little princess knows he wants you to be in control, but trusts you to take him all the way there.

Enter the sculpting classes.

Consider the princess as a ball of clay. If he is a cuckold, that is in very real terms what he is. He is ready, willing, and able to become whatever you need or want to mold him into. This is a somewhat obvious observation but when it is put in such flagrantly blatant terms, it takes on a power of its own.

"I am going to manipulate you." "I want and plan to make you my little cuckold. You can fight, but we both know I will win, so stop fighting and just accept your destiny." "You wanted to be cuckolded. You begged me. Now, I am in control and I will make you become my little sissy partner in crime."

Ya, they all sound a little corny and staged. They are. But you get the point. Don't be ashamed to see your relationship in this light. A cuckold is a perfect gift for girls like us. We get to make them into whatever we want and need.

On that, I don't want to imply the sculpting has to be routed with malicious intent or to be sadistic. Sure, some of those elements may play into the process, but the point is to understand and fear not the position a cuckoldress has. Don't be afraid to acknowledge, accept or reiterate this to your cuckold.

At the very beginning of any cuckold relationship, this is an implied understanding that you both have but with infantile understanding. As you evolve, it will become more evident to both of you. To add spice, a simple reminder to cucky will help you both evolve and grow without barriers of the unspoken.

STEP 10 - REPITITION

⚭

They say repetition is the mother of skill. I say it's the sister of pleasure.

As with almost anything in life, the more you do something, the more comfortable you get with it. The better you get at it. Do something once, you're lucky. Do something 10 times, you must be good. Do something 100's of times, often you're considered an expert.

Cuckolding is exactly that way. That is not my point, however.

Within cuckolding, the sexual pleasure/emotional pain is a dance. You both get better with time. You get better at picking out the right bulls and getting comfortable allowing yourself to get lost in all the sensual pleasures he has. Cucky gets used to the angst, losing control, and the acceptance that this is the way you both truly wanted it to be.

But what if you could speed up that pain/pleasure cycle

of learning for both of you? What if you could make bull #8 feel like bull #47... for both you and cucky?

This is my little backdoor secret, ladies. Repetition.

So moving on...

Wait, what?

Yes, I will elaborate. I think the repetition of living in the lifestyle will help you both grow and get comfortable, but that is something that will happen no matter what. You can't control or accelerate that.

BUT, you can hone into a very specific part of the dynamic that is worth highlighting.

If you find a bull that works for you - respects you, pushes all the right buttons, and is equally interested in repeat episodes. Do not let him go. He is about to become a very key element.

Starting from the top, cuckolding is about you being selfish and having the best sex of your life. We both know, being with a partner that "clicks" is often hard to find. But when it does...

You owe it to yourself. Why go to a different bull when Mr. Big does just fine?

Here's where things get interesting though.

When your little princess sees you repeatedly with the same bull, each time you reach heights of ecstasy that blow the roof off his own performance, what do you think happens?

He gets concerned. He gets perhaps a little more jealous than if it was just some average bull. And if you keep re-visiting the same bull over and over and over, it becomes very clear, you really really want his ass.

To your cuckold, this is the worst / best thing that could happen. They throw his cuckold instincts into overdrive. He will feel all the emotions he normally would, only they are heightened dramatically. By you seeing the same bull multiple times, your cuck will sense a bond developing (which there will be). He will fear the quality of your play session is perhaps "too good" for his comfort. Really? Too good?

Ladies, that's the point. You want the best sex of your life. What better way to find it than by pinning down the bull that just has that something special.

Trust me when I say, this will cause problems, but not colossal problems. When your cuck can no longer stand seeing you with the same man over and over and over, he will say something. If and more likely, when he does, then and ONLY THEN do you move on.

Remember, this kind of repetition is intentional and effective. You are proactively trying to pump up the volume of angst with your little princess. He wants it but also does not. Just have fun, take him to the edge and then let it go. As long as you know what you're doing and why you're doing it, it's all good. If your cucky has issues with this approach, have him read this section after the fact so he knows it was done for his personal growth as a cuckold. You did it because you love him and you know he needs to feel all that good nasty stuff he adores, just like you need to feel all the good stuff that it brings too.

Before I leave this, I just want to add a word of caution. This kind of repetition, although extremely effective, can also be the most slippery step you can take. Almost without exception, this is where davie and I have seen some of our cuckold couple friends lose their place. One of two things has happened. Either the number of times to see a bull was agreed upon much earlier in their relationship (a hardline was established) and the cuckoldress ignored it, forgetting it was a big deal to her little cuck. If this was the case, not cool. HARD LINES ARE NEVER TO BE CROSSED... EVER! She should have discussed it with her cuck, or he should have said he was not comfortable with her repeat visits to one bull.

Sadly, the other biggest reason that it can be a problem is you, the cuckoldress. Sex has huge emotional energy attached. If you find a bull that pushes all your buttons, AND you see this person repeatedly, do not kid yourself. YOU ARE HUMAN. You could develop a real emotional attachment to them. Likewise, they could find they "fall in love" with you... all while your cuckold sits in fear that it may be happening.

Be very careful here. If you or your bull develops feelings for each other, beyond sex, you need to drop them like it's hot. I mean, run far and fast. And DO NOT LOOK BACK. Forget they ever happened and never contact them again. Failure to do that is almost certain to bring complete devastation to your marriage. Remember, cuckolding is a relationship dynamic you and your little princess have formed BECAUSE you love each other so deeply. Repetition of the same bull is awesome but always be careful where your head and the bull's head are at.

STEP 11 - MIX IT UP

☿

D o I mean black, white, latino? Nope (although that works for me). Do I mean doggy, mission- ary, and reverse cowgirl? Nope (also works for me btw). In the spirit of this book, I am specifically refer- ring to mixing up anything and everything that will moti- vate your cuckold to be more attentive, loving, and a compliant little sissy.

Before I say anything else, I should mention the assumption that you have established no hard lines between you and your cuckold in the area we are about to explore. For some cucks, it is a tremendous deal that they are present at all times or this or that. If you and your cuck have set any hard limits, please respect them. If not, let the games begin.

All men are very visual creatures. For the cuck this is not much different. HOWEVER, unlike 99% of the male population, their operating system is a little more devious and complicated.

They traditionally portrayed cuckolding as a sex act by the cuckoldress and the bull IN FRONT OF THE CUCKOLD - sometimes the cuck is restrained, sometimes he is caged, sometimes they force him into engaging with the bull. Rarely is he absent from the playtime.

I would argue that all the above are good and valid but that the cuckold's presence should be seen as a special delight. A treat. A kind of reward for exemplary behavior. In the initial stages of a cuckolding relationship, this area is extremely critical. You both will have crossed that line by the time you get to this point, so I'm assuming if it is an obstacle that is not possible to overcome, skip to the next chapter. If you're still at the threshold of cuckolding altogether, I'd recommend my DNA series that breaks down the complexities of the dynamic in a more clinical way.

With that out of the way, I would encourage you to always keep your cuck on edge. Never lie. NEVER EVER CHEAT. But, always be one step ahead of him on when, how, and where the action will happen. For davie, this was scary at first. It just kind of happened by accident. I was already talking to a bull we had met online. He knew about him and we had met casually for coffee once. The bull suggested we meet at a motel near our home. No problem, right? It was at 1... in the afternoon. Davie was at work.

I texted davie and told him I was going to play with bubba. His response was a dry but submissive "ok". This random hook-up was not planned and up till that point, davie was always with me. I had the bull shoot some video off my phone, take a few photos, and sent them to my princess later in the afternoon.

Davie was at work. Did I mention that? He called me from a bathroom stall to advise he needed to please himself. He could not control the rush. It was that powerful. When he returned home... let's just say I had a VERY GOOD EVENING!

Mixing up the scenarios without your cucky knowing about it (assuming he's okay with it...) will light a fire under his cute baby bum.

Plan to have bulls over with your little one knowing in advance. Have bulls come over without advance notice. Meet bulls when cucky girl is not around, making sure he knows about it first. Also, do this when he does not know about it UNTIL THE VERY LAST MINUTE.

Have him there, watching, and also insist that he remain downstairs and only listen to the groans. Leave the cage on and also give him times to play with himself as he watches or listens.

The point is to keep things moving in all directions at all times. It will keep his heart beating hard and fast (unlike his useless little pee-pee - let's be honest ladies). Also, hold a few random video clips and photos on your phone. They could be from playtimes that your cuck has or has not been a part of. Do not let him become aware of said digital files. When you want to move the dial (for any reason) fire him a few. Make sure he is in a compromised position (at work, with the boys on the golf course, playing at the park with the kids). He will be utterly useless in what he can do with them, but you have just fucked with his mind in the most profound way.

Mix it up and always look for more.

STEP 12 - DEAD END AHEAD

S tepping back to step 2, this is a kind of a subset to it. Using your words.

Using the words that you are a cuckoldress **BECAUSE YOU WANT TO FUCK OTHER MEN INSTEAD OF YOUR CUCK** AND YOU WANT TO SEE HIM BECOME YOUR CUTE LITTLE PRINCESS is the most powerful and sweet words that every cuckold dreams of hearing. **<u>BUT</u>** there is an almost equally powerful set of words when formed into a sentence that has almost the same value and impact.

Ready?

I can't stress this enough. This should be said perhaps as much as "I love you". It will crank little cutie pie up and yet slowly break him down - or at least any man parts he has left.

Cuckolding is no longer an option. It is not a choice. It

is inevitable. It is a requirement for the health and longevity of your marriage/relationship. It is a permanent status, that is and will always be. For you to continue as a couple, he must remain your little cute princess and you must remain his goddess.

The above paragraph or any derivative thereof are the sentiments you want to drill into his head. Do it as often as possible. Every time he hears that message, check his pants. I'm serious. Check them.

Removing the choice for him is half the appeal to cuckolding. Cuckolds are control freaks in the vanilla world. They often have positions of authority where they call the shots, they decide and the fate of others is directly in their hands. They are typically very well educated and can see much of the logic to cuckolding (intellectually) makes no sense. And yet, they just can't help themselves. It pulls them in like a black hole. They don't want to be a cuckold. They love the dynamic more than anything else in the world. It literally completes them.

For you to take this key element of control - the fate of your relationship and to make it fully conditional on the continuation of this cuckold dynamic... it seems like the cruelest thing any woman could do to the man she loves. But, CHECK HIS PANTS.

Yip.

There you go. Welcome to the upside-down world of cuckolding. Much makes no sense but it just works.

Telling your princess it's no longer optional is not cruel. If you really love him and you have both established that cuckolding works for you, it is the most loving, kind, and caring thing you could do. You have helped cucky make a decision he didn't want to make. He wanted you to decide. And here's the kicker...

Secretly, he wanted the decision to be exactly the one you have just told him. Now that is selfless and loving for you to say that if you ask me. This is not a mean, cruel and small deal.

In casual conversation, davie mentioned this to me early in our relationship. I just thought it was odd and never thought that I'd ever find myself saying it or more-over WANTING TO SAY IT and meaning it.

It is now part of our daily ritual salutations beyond the "I love you" and "have a good day, princess." There was no backlash. No negative repercussions. It was not even hard to say, cause that was exactly what I felt.

Now, at the possibility some of my readers may feel reluctant, I challenge you to take time and ask yourself why? For most, it will be a nervous concern that this will irreparably hurt their little man. If that's the case, try it, and if he becomes unglued, pass it off as just a joke. There is room for recovery.

For others, your reluctance may be based on a legiti-mate and solid foundation. Your cuckolding dynamic is either too premature, too unstable or perhaps not working because you or he are only in it to please your partner. If so, that's cool. Don't say it unless you mean it. And if you mean it but your marital intuition tells you your cucky is not really a cuckold, just a guy that wanted to please you, trust that gut instinct and refrain. If your husband/partner is not a cuckold, I'd encourage you to stop before things fall apart completely (because they will). This dynamic only works for a real cuckold and cuckoldress. Yes, anybody can dip their toes in the water to try it. But to make it a relationship dynamic, it just isn't possible for long-term success unless you both have the DNA for it to work.

STEP 13 - KICK HIM WHEN HE'S DOWN

T he lucky Step 13. Seriously. This is a step that I failed to take for a long time and boy, did I pay for it. Every time I would play with my bulls, davie would be all gung-hoe. He'd be my obedient little princess, supportive, attentive, happy, and full of energy. Then, after I was done, I'd see him crash, ESPECIALLY if I allowed him to finish too. He would repeatedly go into these deep, dark dives of emotional angst. It's like depression but more.

Yes, this was early in our relationship and we were both learning things about each other and ourselves, so this was all new and scary to both of us. My instinct when I'd see him fall apart was to comfort him. I would feel guilty that my actions had just plummeted him to feel so sad and desperate.

I would hold him and tell him I loved him and it was all okay that I would never do it again if he wanted me to stop. With each action or word, he would get even more emotional. At first, I wanted to die. I felt like a terrible wife and human. The cycle would repeat, sometimes even when I was playing. He'd just randomly have his dark moments and I would instinctively go into damage control and drop the whole "cuckoldress/goddess" persona and resume my caring vanilla self. And... he almost always would get worse.

What was going on there? Neither of us understood it at the time but as I said earlier, davie was going through Cuckold Angst. It is a necessary, healthy, and essential part of a cuckold dynamic. It is not a bad thing at all. Cuckolding is kind of built around the premise of creating this angst. With davie's little mind, he craves the angst. In my mind, once I understood it, I craved the creation of his angst.

One of these days I need to get davie to help co-author a book around angst cause I don't get what he feels. He's tried to explain it as like a depression mixed with desperation mixed with anger mixed with conflicting flashes of joy and excitement that he likes the negativity as he's feeling it? I don't know. Suffice to say, your little cucky will feel it, AND WHEN HE DOES...

You need to kick him when he's down in that headspace. I mean, this is when angst becomes your best friend. I know it will go against everything that you think and instinctively feel you should do, from a human compassion point of view. I've been there with davie, sitting on the couch where he was crying, feeling so sorry for himself. He wasn't even upset at me, just angry and jealous that he was born with the cuck DNA, and... you'll see if you haven't already.

Here's the part that is so true but feels impossible to get your head around and rationalize. When cucky is suffering from his little angst attacks, the best thing you can do is dig into your goddess status even further. Tell him he is a little sissy. That his behavior is childish and unacceptable. Tell him that his behavior is getting you excited and that you need him to do his "duty" and get on his knees and please you. The colder and more emotionally detached you can make yourself, the quicker he will bounce back to his happy little cucky self.

Doing this while you have your hand on his little pee-pee... you want to see him smile and have a 180-degree shift inside half a second? Ladies, it's like having a key to the magical kingdom. I know it feels so wrong. Cruel even. Try it just once. It will blow your mind how simple and easy pulling him out of his angst can be. Moreover, this is what he wants and needs. The rush of power I feel when I see just how weak he is and how much power and control I have over him is... okay, I have to stop. I'm getting wet.

When he sees you acting all caring, loving, and compassionate, it stresses his pain. There is nothing wrong with loving and tender - BUT NOT WHILE HE'S IN THE MIDDLE OF AN ANGST ATTACK. Wrong, wrong, wrong!

If you love him and want him to cherish you and the gift you have given him in the cuckold experience, you will kick him when he's down. Again, I don't mean to suggest you have a loveless marriage. Quite the contrary. You just need to make sure the loving, tender and caring moments are nowhere close to the times that you're in play or when he's suffering from angst.

STEP 14 - THE NON-UNIVERSAL

⚭

A s with all sexual behaviors, everyone is different. Some people love role play while others think it's stupid and see no value in it. They would rather use whips and handcuffs. No one is wrong. As long as it's consensual and everyone is enjoying it, I say it's fantastic and go for it!

In cuckolding, the same division falls somewhere between disparity and the cuckold, remaining loyal to the cuckoldress. Specifically, in the world of homosexuality.

I pass no judgment on any couple that wants to go this path, HOWEVER, this would be considered a part of the dynamic that falls into the extreme edge of what cuckolding is about. Remember, cuckolding is a relationship dynamic of disparity. A relationship that allows and encourages both partners to allow their sadistic and masochistic sides out and compliment one and other. This is where davie and I sit in our relationship.

For a rather large minority, this expression of S&M in conjunction with homosexual tendencies or interests can lead to an area that is not universal to all cuckold relationships but is a big enough component that I felt I should mention.

Pegging, fluffing, cream-pie cleanup, and "forced" fellatio. They all dance around the idea of your little princess engaging in varying degrees of what would be considered gay behavior with your bull.

I don't want to pretend I have experience in this area because davie and I do not. What I can offer are my thoughts on how, when, and why.

If you sense your cuck wants to go there, talk about it. Do not go there until you know you are both ok with it. I appreciate that half the appeal a cuck gets is with you pushing him beyond his normal limits. This is not an area you want to go to if you don't at least have some inclinations from your spouse.

I would also recommend starting from the place of least impact if things don't go as planned. Pegging (where you have a strap-on) in the privacy of your own home may be an ideal place to start. If things go wrong, it's just the two of you.

Once you have established little cucky would like to "help" with your bull, role play this out privately. You do not want to force your cuck into this if he isn't kind of already willing. If you leave it until playtime, he will probably fluff your bull, eat the bull's cum, and anything else you ask of him. During those moments, he is in a subspace. He is literally incapable of saying no to anything you ask of him - even if he had stated it is on his hard limit list. But the aftermath if it is not his thing will be devastating.

Trust me, you don't want to go there until you have had some dialogue in advance. As with all things cuckolding, if he gives you a green light, then get aggressive. Get him to play with a willing bull, while you go have a cigarette and a drink. Sit and watch your little cuck be a real woman helping his goddess make the bull happy.

Some of our friends have said it has amped up the bond they have as a couple. Your cuck in this situation now becomes an active participant in the sex. It's like you are both on the same team, making the bull happy and making the cuckoldress happy. AND, making the cuck degrade himself to a true sissy. His actions symbolize a loss of his manhood and he is now performing sexual acts like a woman. I think it's cute. It's just not for davie and I, but many of my friends in the lifestyle swear by it. To get your man to drop to such a degrading level is exciting, not going to lie. For davie, it's a line I can't cross.

BONUS TIPS

Here are some simple tips that I've covered elsewhere but are worth mentioning again. Remember, the point of this book is to help you improve your husband's experience or to help him in his transition into the life of being a cuckold. Here are a few that I've found work miracles with davie's need to be cuck'd.

Never shave - EVER... unless it's date night with your bull. Your cuck is your number one, but in the sex department, he is your number zero. Both of you need to know it and feel it.

When it's just you and your little princess, NEVER dress up. Track pants and a sweatshirt/tank top or whatever. Bring on the Granny panties. Sexy outfits - they are only for your bulls. He should only be allowed a small glimpse of what your bulls will take in for an entire evening. The only exception to this is when you want to tease your cuck. Wear his favorite little outfit, hosiery, shoes, make-up, etc, and tease the hell out of him. BUT... when you play this game, these should be the times that he gets nothing from you. He should only be allowed to please you. Let the visual images burn in his brain (mind fucking him). If you are intimate, always aim for the plain Jane look.

Daily exercises. You could call these daily therapy sessions or daily affirmations. I don't know. But this one has evolved for davie and me, only since early 2020 when the world went upside down and we found the time to start this quick, tiny ritual that we both just love. Aim for it to be a once-a-day thing. If you miss a day or two, that's okay, but you want this to become a very regular thing that you will both greatly benefit from. Find some privacy for both of you. If you have kids, the bathroom is a safe bet. Put your hands down his pants. Caged or not, fondle the tiny little guy. He likely will not go hard, at least not initially. Do this for 30 seconds then look directly into his eyes and make two or three statements and ask him to respond out loud. Try to make the statements short, sweet, and most importantly, the same statements made over and over and over.

Statements like: "your little guy is so small and soft. I need a real man. Are you a real man?" - get him to answer.

"I love fucking other men. Tell me. I want to hear you say it. Do you like me fucking other men? Do you want me to fuck other men?" - again, get him to respond.

"I love this life as a cuckoldress. You know why? Because you're a little useless sissy. Aren't you? Are you a little sissy? Do you love being cuckolded, sissy girl?" - get him to answer.

And that's it. Your session is done for the day. Oh, by the way. 100% chance, he's now rock hard. I gotta admit. It's just so damn cute.

Do this repeatedly and you will find he becomes EXTREMELY MOTIVATED to the lifestyle and you will also find any guilt quickly melts away, especially hearing him openly admitting the things that usually are only discussed at infrequent random times. When you make this a daily statement you both openly affirm to each other, it helps bring you both to an emotional and mental headspace where it feels normal and natural as a couple. It makes acceptance of who you really are to each other that much easier.

One final bonus tip has been intentionally left to the very end. The cage. The cock cage (or male chastity belt). I have left this out as an entire chapter because I have discussed this in detail in my DNA books and I also feel this tool is discussed so often in so much material that it kind of seems like overkill at this point. That being said, it does work, and it has extreme value if used properly. Once the novelty of having cucky having one wears off, you'll realize its true function is to stabilize his massive fluctuations in testosterone. When sissy is not allowed to relieve himself, his need for a release climbs. And climbs. And climbs. The more the need, the more he will do anything for you. The more compliant, loving, and attentive he becomes. This is all good and necessary - especially in the earlier stages of a cuckold relationship.

As time progresses, however, you don't want his life to depend on being locked up 24/7. It's cruel and physically unhealthy. Think of the cage as a training tool and a means of punishment more than a way to stress the cuck experience. To repeat, it is a great place to start, but make sure you put its use in its proper perspective. Too much of a good thing here can be toxic to his health (physically AND EMOTIONALLY).

FINAL THOUGHTS

Nothing about cuckolding is a self-contained, individual activity. Although many aspects of this kind of relationship can feel like you are both miles apart (and sometimes, literally are), it is a dynamic like no other. It bonds you to a level of the soul. Everything is about you as a couple. Yes, I have sex with my bulls and get taken to heights davie can never take me, but I love my little sissy. I want to make this the front of your mind. Everything I've suggested here is coming from a place of love, kindness, devotion, and appreciation for davie. He is my everything. Nothing I have done was done in an unethical or sinister way to manipulate him in a non-consensual way.

On the surface, to an outsider, some of what I've said could be viewed this way. But that's to AN OUTSIDER that has no real understanding of what a cuckold dynamic is all about. If you were to ask davie, he would tell you I'm the best thing that has ever happened to him. That everything I've done has been deeply appreciated and has enriched his life at a level he too never thought possible.

Remember, to a true cuckold, the sexiest, most loving, and amazing thing you could ever possibly do to him is to deny him. Tease him with no reward, humiliate and degrade everything about his manhood. Making him feel loved (at the appropriate times) but utterly useless sexually, is his ultimate dream.

Similarly, to a true cuckoldress, the dreams and desires of a cuckold are almost too good to be true. To be allowed and encouraged to stop being Miss Goody Goody and let the darker side feel free to dance and grow. To never feel guilty, all the while knowing your cuckold loves the emotional pain and you love giving him that pain - all guilt-free.

This, my readers are the magic ingredients that makes this dynamic so special and why it works so friggen well. It is a match made in heaven.

If I was to offer a single statement that captures the overall essence of this book and what a cuckoldress needs to do to help move the needle and get her cuckold in his happy place, it would be this: As a cuckoldress, you are free and single to have sex with ANYONE YOU WANT. THE MORE YOU ACT AND THINK THIS WAY, THE MORE YOUR CUCKY WORSHIPS YOU AND WANTS TO SHARE THIS LIFESTYLE. He WANTS YOU to act and TO THINK that way. I know right. Admittedly, it sounds messed up, but I'm telling you, cuck olding is a mind fuck.

The thing is, the more I have followed the above path... the more I do it... the more davie loves me and the more I feel free, empowered, and like I'm back in my early 20s. It's a fucking amazing life we now share and we both win, feeding on each other's needs and deepest and darkest desires. I wouldn't trade it for the world.

I want you to finish this book knowing and feeling confident that everything I've suggested should not make you feel guilty or like you're a bad person for doing it... or even wanting to do it. I have found that my actions have profoundly helped davie live a deeply satisfying life filled with love and passion at levels neither one of us could have ever felt if we had stayed in the vanilla world.

Every ounce of your selfishness and sexual energy on other men will leave your cuck suspended in true euphoria. He loves you deeply and is good to you. By using some of the steps contained here, you strengthen that bond, that love, that insatiable need. You deserve to be fucked properly. Let's be real girls. The harsh truth is, if your hubby is a true cuck, it's just never gonna happen. **You deserve the life of a cuckoldress.** If you really love him, **he deserves the life of a tiny cucky boy**. It will rock your worlds beyond your wildest dreams.

While I still have your attention, I just want to thank you so much for your time. It brings davie and me great pleasure and satisfaction knowing we are helping other couples come over to the "dark side". If you found this book helpful, please give it a rating in whatever book retailer you got it from. Even better, leave a comment. The more people that shout out, the easier it is for other like-minded folks to find this kind of material.

Again, thank you so much.

H ugs and kisses,
A & d

ALSO BY ALLORA SINCLAIR

ABOUT THE AUTHOR

ABOUT THE AUTHOR

 Allora Sinclair is a happily married 40 year old mom. She and her loving cuckold husband Dave (davie) have been in a cuckold marriage for over seven years and she has now decided to start documenting their journey. If Allora is not found at her computer or out shopping for a new pair of shoes, she is usually found in the caring arms of davie or embraced in ecstasy with one of her favorite bulls. She has done a series of non-fiction books to help couples navigate their way through the heavily distorted life of being a cuckold couple. She has also worked on a series of fiction books that are loosely based on some of their real-life adventures. If you found this book to be of value, please be sure to rate it or leave a comment with the book retailer you got it from.

Printed in Great Britain
by Amazon

36398224R00035